THE POCKET TIMELINE OF
Ancient Greece

Emma McAllister

UNIVERSITY PRESS

Published in association with The British Museum

Emma McAllister has asserted the right to be identified as the author of this work.

Published in the United States of America by
Oxford University Press, Inc.
198 Madison Avenue
New York, NY 10016
www.oup.com

Oxford is a registered trademark of Oxford University Press, Inc.

Oxford University Press, Inc., publishes works that further Oxford University's objective of excellence in research, scholarship, and education.

Library of Congress Cataloging-in-Publication data is available

ISBN-13:   978-0-19-530128-1
ISBN-10:   0-19-530128-5

Designed and typeset by Peter Bailey at Proof Books
Printed in China

CONTENTS

EARLY GREECE

7000 TO 1100 BC GREECE IS A mountainous land, almost completely encircled by the Mediterranean Sea. It is surrounded by well over a thousand islands. The first farmers settled there around 7000 BC. We know very little about these early settlers. However, during the Bronze Age (3200 – 1100 BC) two great civilizations came into existence in Greece.

The Minoan civilization emerged around 3200 BC on Crete. The Minoans were not Greek and may have originally come from western Asia. The civilization grew wealthy through trade with countries such as Egypt, Asia Minor and the Levant. They built great palaces from which they ruled the island. Excavations show that these palaces were beautifully decorated with wall-paintings. The Minoans were skilled artists and craftsmen, creating many beautiful objects.

Minoan storage jar, found in the palace of Knossos.

Minoan gold pendant.

A room in the Minoan palace of Knossos.

The Mycenaean civilization flourished on mainland Greece from around 1600 BC. It was a warlike society. Their citadels were surrounded by huge, thick walls for defence. The Mycenaeans traded with Egypt, Asia Minor, Italy and Cyprus. They were very wealthy and archaeologists have uncovered many objects in gold, silver and ivory from their towns. Around 1450 BC the Mycenaeans expanded into Crete and came under the influence of Minoan culture. Their writing system, called 'Linear B', was adapted from a Minoan script. Unlike the Minoans, the Mycenaeans spoke Greek. They also worshipped some of the same gods as Greeks many hundreds of years later.

Minoan bronze model of an acrobat jumping over a bull. Bulls were an important symbol to the Minoans. Bull-jumping is shown frequently in Minoan art.

Tablets inscribed with 'Linear B' script.

Mycenaean mixing bowl, showing a scene of war or hunting.

THE DARK AGE AND GEOMETRIC PERIOD

Pottery box with Geometric decoration.

1100 TO 700 BC

THE MYCENAEAN civilization collapsed some time after 1200 BC. After this, Greece was plunged into a 'Dark Age'. Writing was no longer used. Trade with other countries went into a steep decline. Very little is known about this time, but it seems that the population of Greece became much smaller.

Signs of widespread recovery in Greece came in the 9th century BC. A number of independent cities began to emerge in Greece. In Athens, a new style of pottery was created. It was decorated with lines,

Mixing bowl, made during the Geometric Period. It shows a man and woman boarding a ship with rows of oarsmen.

zig-zags and other rectilinear patterns. In the 8th century BC humans and animals began to be portrayed in Greek art. These figures were shown in a very simplified and angular way. Historians call this time (900 – 700 BC) the Geometric Period.

Trade with other countries began to increase slowly. The Phoenicians were important trading partners. They came from an area on the eastern Mediterranean coast which is now part of Lebanon and Syria. The Greeks adapted the Phoenician writing system to create their own alphabet. This alphabet is the basis of the writing system we use today.

During the 8th century BC many of the cities of Greece sent their citizens out to create settlements in other lands. These Greek settlements, known as colonies, were set up in countries such as France, Egypt, Italy, Sicily, Libya and the lands around the Black Sea.

Wine bowl with Geometric patterns.

A bronze horse made during the Geometric Period.

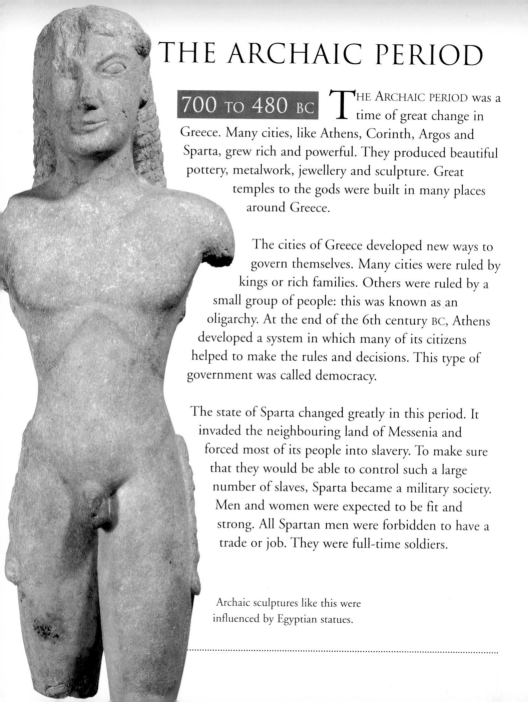

THE ARCHAIC PERIOD

700 TO 480 BC THE ARCHAIC PERIOD was a time of great change in Greece. Many cities, like Athens, Corinth, Argos and Sparta, grew rich and powerful. They produced beautiful pottery, metalwork, jewellery and sculpture. Great temples to the gods were built in many places around Greece.

The cities of Greece developed new ways to govern themselves. Many cities were ruled by kings or rich families. Others were ruled by a small group of people: this was known as an oligarchy. At the end of the 6th century BC, Athens developed a system in which many of its citizens helped to make the rules and decisions. This type of government was called democracy.

The state of Sparta changed greatly in this period. It invaded the neighbouring land of Messenia and forced most of its people into slavery. To make sure that they would be able to control such a large number of slaves, Sparta became a military society. Men and women were expected to be fit and strong. All Spartan men were forbidden to have a trade or job. They were full-time soldiers.

Archaic sculptures like this were influenced by Egyptian statues.

Despite the differences between the Greek cities, they all shared the same religion. During the Archaic Period, festivals were held where people from all over Greece could come together to worship the gods. The most famous and important of these festivals was the Olympic Games.

Many of the Greek cities joined together when faced with a common enemy. At the beginning of the fifth century BC Greece was invaded twice by the Persians. The Persians ruled over a vast empire which stretched from modern Iran to Turkey. Even though the Greeks were greatly outnumbered, they were able to drive the invaders from their land.

Gold model of a Persian chariot from the 5th or 4th century BC.

The temple of Apollo at Corinth, built in the 6th century BC.

THE GODS OF MOUNT OLYMPUS

The ancient Greeks believed that there were a great number of gods and goddesses. These gods had control over many different things on earth. Poseidon controlled the sea. Eros could cause people to fall in love by one hit from his arrow. Demeter could cause crops and plants to grow or die.

In many ways the Greek gods were very human. They could be kind or mean, angry or pleasant, cruel or loving. They fell in love with each other, argued with each other and even stole from each other!

Statue of Demeter, the goddess of farming and fertility.

Poseidon, god of the sea, painted on a drinking cup.

King of all the gods and goddesses was Zeus. He could control the weather and was called 'the thunderer' or 'the cloud-gatherer'.

Aphrodite, goddess of love.

Zeus lived with the other gods on Mount Olympus, a high mountain in northern Greece.

The ancient Greeks built great temples and sanctuaries to their gods. They held festivals in their honour, with processions, sports, sacrifices and competitions. Stories of the gods' lives were told to children by their mothers and to large audiences by professional bards and storytellers. People today still enjoy hearing stories about the Greek gods.

Vase showing Zeus, the king of the gods, holding a thunderbolt.

The Hephaisteion in Athens, a temple dedicated to the god Hephaistos and the goddess Athena.

THE OLYMPIC GAMES

The first recorded Olympic Games were held in 776 BC. This was the most important festival in the ancient Greek calendar. The five-day festival was dedicated to the god Zeus. Athletes from all over the Greek world travelled to Olympia in the hope of becoming sporting heroes. It was such an important festival that wars were suspended so that people could travel there in safety.

The ancient Greeks believed that sport was a very good way to honour the gods. Many religious festivals included athletic competitions. Winners were treated like heroes and brought great glory to their family and home towns. Athletes trained and competed naked. They worked for years before the Games with a personal trainer.

The chariot race was one of the most dangerous events in the Games. There were many accidents and collisions, especially when chariots made the sharp turn at either end of the racecourse.

These athletes are taking part in a sport called the *pankration*. It was like wrestling, but with very few rules. In fact, the only thing that was not allowed in a game was biting your opponent, or trying to gouge his eyes out! On this vase it looks as if one of the competitors is breaking the rules of the game.

Only men were allowed to participate in the games. Women were not allowed even to watch the sports. Events included running, chariot racing, horse racing, wrestling and boxing.

The Olympic Games were held every four years until Roman times. The Games were banned in AD 393 because the Christian rulers of Greece did not want a festival that honoured pagan gods to continue. However, in the 19th century AD there was renewed interest in ancient Greek culture. The Olympic Games were revived in Athens in 1896. The modern Olympic Games are held every four years in a different city around the world.

Winners at the Olympic Games were presented with ribbons and a crown of olive leaves.

This statue shows an athlete about to throw a discus. Discus-throwing is still an event in the modern Olympics.

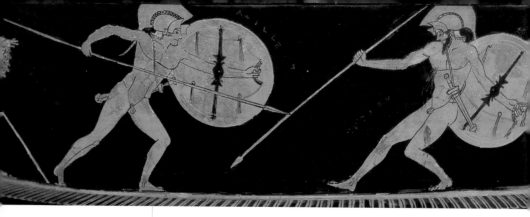

Achilles and Hektor (two heroes of the Trojan War) in battle.

HOMER

Homer was a storyteller who lived some time in the 8th century BC. He created two of the most popular and enduring stories ever told, *The Iliad* and *The Odyssey*.

The Iliad is a story set in the last year of the Trojan War. It tells of the deeds of the heroes and gods who fought in this terrible war between the Greeks and the Trojans. *The Odyssey* follows the hero Odysseus and his many adventures on the journey home from the Trojan War.

The Trojan War was a legendary battle between an alliance of Greek cities and the city of Troy in modern Turkey. The war is said to have begun when Paris, a Trojan prince, ran away with Helen, the wife of King Menelaus of Sparta.

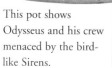

This pot shows Odysseus and his crew menaced by the bird-like Sirens.

Marble bust of Homer, made in the 1st or 2nd century AD.

14

THE PERSIAN WARS

In the early 5th century BC the Persian empire, one of the great powers in the world, launched an attack on Greece. The Persian army landed at Marathon, 40 km (26 miles) north of Athens. The Persian army greatly outnumbered the Athenians. However, the Athenian generals were cunning and outwitted their enemies. The Persians were defeated and lost almost 64,000 soldiers during the battle.

The modern marathon race gets its name from the Battle of Marathon. A messenger was sent from Marathon to announce the victory in Athens. He ran the 40 km (26 miles) in just three hours. The effort proved too much for him and he dropped dead afterwards.

Ten years later the Persians had a new king, Xerxes. He launched another attack on Greece. The Persians moved through the north of Greece, destroying everyone and everything in their path. Athens was almost reduced to rubble by the invaders. The Persians were eventually halted by the Athenian navy at Salamis. At the Battle of Plataia the Greek city states united to drive the Persians out of Greece for good.

Greek warriors wore bronze armour and used a short sword and long spear in battle.

Bronze helmet and greaves (leg guards).

THE CLASSICAL PERIOD

480 TO 323 BC THE CLASSICAL PERIOD was a 'Golden Age' for ancient Greek culture. Literature, philosophy, art and architecture all flourished. Artists and sculptors portrayed people and animals in a natural and realistic way. Philosophers such as Sokrates, Plato and Aristotle tried to find explanations for how the world worked. Playwrights wrote great dramas that were enjoyed by thousands and are still performed today.

Athens and Sparta were the most powerful Greek city states for most of the Classical period. The two cities spent many years at war and Athens was finally defeated in 404 BC. Thebes then became Sparta's main rival in Greece. These cities clashed a number of times during the 4th century BC.

Statuette of the philosopher Sokrates.

A Classical bronze sculpture of the god Apollo.

Soon, most of the Greek cities were very weak because of constant warfare.

The small kingdom of Macedon, in the north of Greece, was able to take advantage of the cities' weakness. King Philip II of Macedon was a great military leader and by 338 BC he had conquered most of Greece. After Philip II died, his son, Alexander the Great, expanded his territory. Alexander ruled over an area that reached from Greece into Egypt and as far east as India. The Classical Period ends with the death of Alexander in 323 BC.

Red figure pottery like this was perfected during the Classical Period.

This Classical relief sculpture shows an army attacking a city.

ATHENS

Athens was one of the most important and powerful Greek cities in the Classical Period. During the Persian Wars, Athens built a very powerful navy and became the greatest naval power in the Greek world. It used its dominance at sea to head a league of Greek cities in the eastern Mediterranean. This league soon became an Athenian empire.

The city was also a great centre for art and literature. Writers, artists and philosophers flocked to the city where they could work and think in freedom. The first university was founded here by the philosopher Plato. For many centuries afterwards, anyone interested in learning would go to Athens to study.

Athens had been left in ruins after the Persian War. The statesman Perikles devised a rebuilding programme for the city. Many beautiful and impressive buildings were constructed in Athens during this time. The most famous of these buildings was the Parthenon. This

The goddess Athena was the patron of the city of Athens.

This silver Athenian coin from 480 BC shows the head of Athena on one side and her symbol, the owl, on the other.

The Parthenon.

temple was covered in painted sculptures made by some of the best craftsmen in Greece and was dedicated to the goddess Athena.

Athena was the patron goddess of Athens. Each year a great festival, called the *Panathenaia*, was held in her honour. Every four years the festival would have a great procession to the Acropolis, the sacred area of the city. Here, a newly-woven gown would be offered to an ancient statue of Athena.

This sculpture comes from the Parthenon. It shows a scene from the procession of the Panathenaia festival. The cow is being led to the Acropolis, where it will be sacrificed to Athena.

A *dikast* ticket. An Athenian citizen would present this at a court of law to show that he could serve on the jury.

Bronze figure of an African slave.

DEMOCRACY IN ATHENS

Athens was the first city to develop democracy. Democracy means that all citizens has a say in how a state or city is governed. Many countries today, including the United Kingdom and the United States, are democracies.

All decisions in Athens had to be voted for by a majority of the people. Citizens voted in an area of the city called the Pnyx. It could hold thousands of people and every citizen had a right to have their say.

However, not everyone in Athens was allowed to take part in the democracy. Only male citizens had the right to vote. This meant that women and children could not take part in government. Athens was also home to thousands of foreigners (known as *metics*) and slaves, and neither of these groups was allowed to vote.

A bust of Perikles, the great statesman who helped to strengthen democracy in Athens.

SPARTA

Sparta was a very different type of city to all the others in Greece. Spartan society was geared towards producing great warriors. Boys aged seven were sent away from their families to train to be soldiers and they did not return home until they were grown men. Their training was very difficult. They were often flogged and beaten so badly they would pass out. Spartans thought this type of cruelty made the boys tough and able to endure anything.

Spartan women had a lot more freedom than other women in Greece. They trained in athletics. The Spartans believed that women had to be fit and strong so that they would give birth to powerful warriors.

Very few artefacts have been found from Sparta from the Classical period. All luxury crafts and arts were outlawed; all energies were poured into creating a strong army.

Bronze figurine from Sparta showing a girl running.

Bronze figure of a Spartan warrior.

These men at a *symposion* recline on couches. After eating and drinking a great deal some of the men fell asleep on these comfortable couches.

IN THE HOME

Houses in Greek cities were very simple. They were made of mud bricks and had tiled roofs. The rooms of the house were arranged around a courtyard. There would be an altar in the courtyard where the family could make sacrifices to the gods.

Respectable Greek women were not supposed to leave their homes much. They spent their time caring for the children, cleaning, cooking, spinning and weaving. The women's rooms (the *gynaekeion*) were often upstairs – as far away as possible from strangers and passers-by.

Wool-working was a very important activity for the home. It provided clothing for all the family and extra cloth could be sold at the market for

This vase shows a *herm*. A herm is a column-like statue of the god Hermes. It was often placed on the porch of a Greek house to keep away evil spirits.

money. Greek clothes were mostly made from wool. The wool was spun very fine so that it would be cool in the heat. Men and women wore simple clothes made out of a rectangle of material that could be fastened at the shoulders and tied at the waist.

Men used their homes to entertain their friends. In the dining room, or *andrôn*, men held banquets called *symposia*. Women were forbidden to attend. However, slave girls were employed to entertain the men. They would dance, play music and do acrobatics.

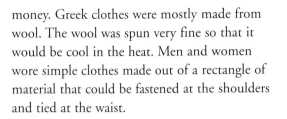

A woman spinning wool.

A woman and her maid looking after a child.

Terracotta figure of a woman making bread.

These toys were found in the grave of a young Greek girl.

CHILDREN

The first few days of a child's life were very important. If a baby did not look healthy the father could leave the baby in a public place. Another family could then adopt the child, but if this did not happen, the baby was left to die.

Growing up in Greece was very different for boys and girls. Boys were sent to school to learn reading, writing and arithmetic. When they reached the age of 12 they would also attend a gymnasium. Here they would train in sports and athletics.

Girls did not go to school. They stayed at home and were trained in housekeeping, child-care and wool-working. These were the skills they would need when they became wives and mothers. Girls in ancient Greece were married quite young, normally at 13 or 14 years old, to husbands often twice their age.

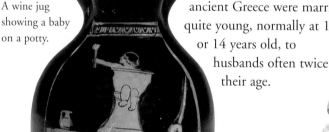

A wine jug showing a baby on a potty.

Statuette of a little girl holding a goose.

This water jar shows an ancient Greek music lesson.

Childhood ended for both boys and girls at the age of 13. To show they were now adults, boys and girls would collect all their toys and leave them at the temple. Boys would dedicate their toys to the god Apollo. Girls would dedicate their toys to the goddess Artemis.

This type of wine jug is called a *chous*. These jars were presented to young boys at a festival called the Anthesteria. During this festival the boys would taste wine for the first time.

Vase showing a boy practising discus-throwing with his trainer.

THEATRE

Drama and theatre were Greek inventions. The ancient Greeks held great festivals in which many plays were performed. At the end of the festival judges would select one of the plays as the winner.

The two main types of play performed were tragedy and comedy. Tragedies dealt with terrible events like war or murder. Often they recreated famous Greek myths and legends. A comedy poked fun at current events and people.

Many thousands of people would attend these festivals, which were dedicated to the god Dionysos. Theatres were built in a special way so that even those at the very back could hear what was being said. Only men were allowed to act. They wore masks to show the audience what type of character they were playing.

Pot showing a scene from a Greek comic play.

Terracotta model of a Greek actor in a mask.

The theatre at Epidauros.

ALEXANDER THE GREAT

The story of Alexander the Great's life seems like that of a mythical Greek hero. He was a great military leader and was known for his courage and bravery. Many believed that he was a descendant of the hero Herakles (whom the Romans called Hercules). Another legend says that he was the son of Zeus. Alexander's army were so loyal to him they would follow him anywhere. He also won the respect of the people he conquered. The wife and mother of the defeated Persian king followed him devotedly. The king's mother even tried to kill herself when Alexander died.

He died aged just 33, thousands of miles away from his home in Macedon. In the thirteen years of his reign he created an empire that stretched from Greece to India and included Egypt. Although his life was short, the world was never the same again because of Alexander.

Marble head of Alexander the Great.

This coin shows Alexander wearing ram's horns, like the Egyptian god Amun. Alexander conquered Egypt in 332 BC.

THE HELLENISTIC PERIOD

323 TO 31 BC T HE HELLENISTIC Period was the time from the death of Alexander the Great to the beginning of the Roman empire. After his death, Alexander's empire was divided up between his generals. The Greek world was now dominated by large kingdoms ruled by dynasties rather than individual city states. The Antigonid dynasty ruled Macedonia, the Seleukids ruled Syria and the Ptolemies ruled Egypt.

Coin issued by Seleucus I, who controlled the eastern portion of Alexander's empire after Alexander's death.

This was a time when Greek influence spread throughout a great deal of the world. The countries that Alexander had conquered adopted the Greek language, religion and styles of art, often mixing them with local traditions. Greek towns with gymnasia, temples and theatres were built in all parts of the empire, even as far away as Afghanistan. In Alexandria in Egypt a great library was built where many of the greatest works of Greek literature and philosophy were collected and preserved.

Coin issued by Ptolemy II. The Ptolemies ruled Egypt after Alexander's death. They were descended from the first Ptolemy, a Greek general in Alexander's army.

Terracotta group of 'knucklebones' players, *c.* 330 – 300 BC. 'Knucklebones' was a popular game in ancient Greece. You had to throw the bones up in the air and then catch as many as possible in one hand.

THE GREEK LEGACY

G REECE BECAME A Roman province in 146 BC.
However, many Greek ideas lived on in the
Roman empire. The Romans greatly admired the
achievements of the Greeks. They adopted Greek
styles of art and architecture. Roman religion shared
the same gods as the Greeks, although they were
called different names.

We are still influenced by the ideas of the ancient
Greeks today. Many of the words we use today
come from the Ancient Greek language. Our type
of government is influenced by the democratic
system of ancient Athens. Buildings like the British
Museum in London copy the style of ancient Greek
architecture. In fact, any time you go to the theatre,
attend a gym or watch the Olympics you are
following in the footsteps of the ancient Greeks.

A Roman copy of a
4th-century BC
Greek sculpture.

The British Museum.

WHO'S WHO

THE ACHIEVEMENTS of the ancient Greeks have lived on for thousands of years. Here are a few of the people whose work and ideas are still valued today.

Aristophanes *c.* 448 – 385 BC. A playwright. He wrote comedies which poked fun at some of Athens' most important and respected people.

Aristotle *c.* 384 – 322 BC. A philosopher. He was a pupil of Plato and later became teacher to Alexander the Great. He developed his theories by observing and recording evidence from the world around him.

Euclid *c.* 300 BC. A mathematician. He made a number of important discoveries in geometry – the study of shapes, lines and points. His book, *Elements*, was one of the first maths books to be printed.

Euripides *c.* 480 – 407/6 BC. A playwright in the 5th century BC. He created tragedies and Aristotle called him the greatest of all the tragedians.

Herodotos *c.* 485 – 425 BC. He is often called 'the father of history' because he was the first historian. He collected stories on his many travels around the Greek world and wrote a history of the Persian War.

Euripides.